The Sa

VEGETARIAN COOKING

Carole Handslip

CONTENTS

Published exclusively for
J Sainsbury plc
Stamford Street, London SE1 9LL
by Cathay Books
59 Grosvenor Street, London W1

First published 1985

ISBN 0 86178 315 8

Printed in Hong Kong

INTRODUCTION

There are several reasons for taking up a vegetarian diet. In the past, the most obvious was the dislike of breeding animals for slaughter. But now, with our increased dietary knowledge, more people are changing their eating habits simply because they know it's better for them. Such is the increased interest in vegetarian and whole foods that most are now readily available in supermarkets.

Nowadays most vegetarians base their diet on whole food – foods to which nothing has been added or taken away. They retain as much of their natural goodness as possible, are not processed or refined and are therefore much better for us.

A lacto vegetarian is one who excludes the use of meat, fish and poultry. A strict vegetarian or Vegan also excludes dairy produce, such as milk, eggs and cheese.

You may find it difficult to cut out meat, fish and poultry all at once, especially before you have become skilled at preparing the alternatives. Indeed, you may not wish to become a strict vegetarian – but simply want to reduce the amount of meat you eat.

To start with, just try to include two or three vegetarian meals each week. As you and your family begin to acquire the taste for vegetarian food, you can gradually omit more animal protein from your diet.

The recipes in this book are for those seeking to explore the delights of vegetarian cookery and to give fresh ideas to those who are already confirmed vegetarians.

NOTES

Standard spoon measurements are used in all recipes
1 tablespoon = one 15 ml spoon
1 teaspoon = one 5 ml spoon
All spoon measures are level.

Ovens should be preheated to the specified temperature.

Use freshly ground black pepper where pepper is specified and sea salt, if preferred, where salt is stated.

Fresh herbs are used unless otherwise stated. If unobtainable substitute a bouquet garni of the equivalent dried herbs, or use dried herbs instead but halve the quantities stated.

For all recipes, quantities are given in both metric and imperial measures. Follow either set but not a mixture of both, because they are not interchangeable.

Use size 3 eggs unless otherwise stated.

Ingredients marked with an asterisk are explained on pages 8-11.

WHY VEGETARIAN?

Vegetarianism is certainly a healthier way of eating. Many of our Western diseases are of recent origin and diet-related. Too great an intake of animal fats, salt and sugar leads to a dramatic increase in the incidence of heart disease, diabetes and obesity, while other diseases, such as diverticulitis and cancer of the bowel, are directly related to lack of fibre in the diet. There is also growing concern as to the effect that preservatives, flavourings and colourings have on health.

An increase in the consumption of fresh vegetables and foods rich in plant protein at the expense of animal protein helps to prevent these 'civilized diseases'.

ALTERNATIVE FOODS

Meat, poultry and fish are prime sources of the protein essential to health, so the vegetarian must seek alternative sources. These can be found in nuts, seeds, legumes (beans and pulses) and, to a lesser extent, in whole grains. These sources also contain fibre, which plays an essential part in the way the body handles the food we eat, but they do not contain the saturated animal fats which are harmful to health.

Vegetarian recipes do not necessarily require the use of whole foods, but they have been used throughout this book in preference to processed foods. Whilst individual ingredients may sometimes appear expensive, it is far cheaper to eat nuts, fruit and vegetables than meat!

When adopting this new way of eating, you must ensure that you achieve a properly balanced diet. There are four main food groups within a vegetarian diet: beans, nuts and seeds; grains; dairy produce; and fruit and vegetables. If you include something from each group in your daily diet you will be sure of getting all the nutrients you need.

PLANNING MEALS

Embarking on a new style of eating will inevitably mean more time spent in the planning and preparation of meals at first. It is in fact no more difficult to cook vegetarian food than any other, but it will take a little time to become accustomed to new methods and to know which foods are best served together.

Try to include a different grain, bean or pulse dish whenever possible so that you discover different combinations of flavours and textures. In particular, it is important to remember that you are no longer tied to the traditional 'meat and 2 veg' concept. Vegetarian cookery is a rich and varied cuisine, full of many

marvellous dishes with definite characteristics. It encompasses many foreign specialities and may comprise of several equally important courses or several dishes served at once. The following guidelines are useful:

- Use wholewheat flour and pasta and brown rice – all of which have more flavour than their white equivalents.
- Breadcrumbs, preferably wholewheat, are used in many recipes and it is a good idea to keep a supply in the freezer for use at a moment's notice.
- Beans are used extensively, so cook large quantities, bag them in usable portions and freeze; they'll then be ready for use within an hour.
- Always keep the water in which you have boiled vegetables for use as a stock. For extra flavour use shoyu (see page 11), yeast extract or vegetable concentrates.

SPECIAL INGREDIENTS

Beans

Beans contain plenty of protein, iron and potassium, and they are the best source of vegetable fibre. There are more than 20 different types of peas and beans, all of which can be sprouted. The mung bean is the most common sprouted bean, producing the familiar bean sprouts.

All beans should be soaked, then drained and rapidly boiled in fresh liquid for 10 minutes at the start of cooking.

Buckwheat

Buckwheat, also known as 'saracen corn', is the seed of a herbaceous plant. It is rich in protein and iron. It is available from healthfood stores, in the form of flour, groats or roasted buckwheat called 'kasha'.

Cheese

Most hard cheeses are made with animal rennet, but a number of vegetarian cheeses are now available and many of the softer cheeses, such as cottage cheese, Ricotta and Feta, are made without rennet.

Dried Fruits

Dried fruits provide protein, iron, calcium, vitamin A and several B vitamins. Many dried fruits, such as apricots, pears, peaches and apples, are treated with sulphur dioxide to help keep

their colour. To remove this, boil the fruit in water for 1 minute before use and discard the water. Most dried fruit is sprayed or dipped in preservative to give a moist appearance; remove this coating by washing the fruit in hot water. Dried fruits that are free from these treatments are available, though of course they are more expensive.

Grains
Grains or cereals are probably the most important staple food in the world. Wheat, rice, barley, oats, millet, rye, and maize are the major food grains. If eaten whole and unrefined they provide valuable fibre in the diet, as well as protein, calcium, iron, phosphorus and potassium.

Lentils
Lentils are one of the oldest crops, cultivated since prehistoric times. They are grown all over the Middle East and India. Of the many varieties, the most common are the green or continental lentils, and brown or split red lentils. They do not need to be soaked before use, though it will shorten the cooking time if they are. Split red lentils are shelled and have therefore lost some of their fibre.

ABOVE: *Red kidney beans, black eye beans, mung beans, chick peas, black beans, butter beans, buckwheat, buckwheat flour, Ricotta cheese, chèvre.*
BELOW: *Prunes, dried apples, dried apricots, figs, pot barley, porridge oats, bulgur wheat, wholewheat, red lentils, green lentils.*

Nuts and Seeds

Nuts and seeds are a high protein food, rich in B vitamins and minerals. Their high fat content is rich in linoleic acid.

Oils and Fats

Oils are one of the essentials of our diet, containing lecithin, vitamins A, E and K, and minerals. Fats and oils can be divided into three kinds: saturated, mono-unsaturated and polyunsaturated. Animal fats, which are solid at room temperature, are high in saturated fats. Excessive consumption of these fats is associated with heart disease. Most vegetable oils are high in polyunsaturated oils. These are preferable because they tend to lower the level of cholesterol in the blood. Polyunsaturated oils include safflower, sunflower, sesame and corn oil. Olive oil is mono-unsaturated and can be regarded as neutral. Margarine, despite its labelling 'high in polyunsaturates', contains at least 50 per cent saturated fat. It is, however, preferable to butter which contains only 3 per cent polyunsaturates.

Sesame Salt

Sesame salt or 'Gomasio' is a good alternative to salt. It is available in healthfood shops but can be made by grinding 5 parts roasted sesame seeds with 1 part salt.

Sea Vegetables

Seaweed is one of the oldest crops. There are many varieties, the most common being Arame, Kombu, Wakame, Dulse and Nori. They are very high in vitamins, essential amino acids and trace elements, especially iodine.

Agar Agar is obtained from several different seaweeds and is used as a substitute for animal gelatine.

Soy Sauce/Shoyu

Naturally fermented soy sauce made from soya beans with wheat or barley is known as 'shoyu'. The manufactured soy sauce usually contains sugar and other additives. Shoyu makes an excellent flavouring for soups, stews, sauces and dressings and as it is quite salty allows you to cut down on added salt. Soy sauce can be used but the flavour will not be as strong.

Tahini

Tahini is a sesame seed paste widely used in the Middle East. It is useful as a flavouring in dips and sauces and can be used as a binding agent in rissoles and nut roasts.

Tofu

Tofu is soya bean curd. Its high protein content makes it a nutritional substitute for meat, fish and dairy products. It is also rich in iron, calcium and B vitamins. Tofu is a versatile ingredient: it can be stir-fried, deep-fried, marinated and added to dressings and sauces. It is available from healthfood stores as lightly pressed 'silken tofu', and 'firm tofu' which is more heavily pressed. Regular tofu has a texture in between the two.

Yogurt

Yogurt is a popular fermented milk product. It is very easily digested, especially goats' milk yogurt, and people who are allergic or sensitive to milk are often able to tolerate yogurt.

ABOVE: *Brazil nuts, hazelnuts, cashews, pumpkin seeds, roasted sesame seeds, whole mixed nuts, safflower oil, corn oil, olive oil, sesame salt, sesame seeds.*
BELOW: *Wakame, Nori, Arame, soy sauce, tahini, tofu, yogurt.*

CHILLED YOGURT AND MINT SOUP

300 g (10 oz) natural yogurt
150 ml (1/4 pint) tomato juice
300 ml (1/2 pint) milk
1 clove garlic, crushed
1 small cucumber, peeled and finely diced
2 tablespoons chopped mint
salt and pepper
mint sprigs to garnish

Place the yogurt and tomato juice in a bowl and mix together thoroughly. Stir in the milk, garlic, cucumber, most of the chopped mint, and salt and pepper to taste. Chill for 2 hours.

Pour the soup into a tureen, and sprinkle with the remaining mint. Garnish with mint sprigs to serve.

Serves 4

CHESTNUT SOUP

1 tablespoon oil
1 onion, chopped
2 celery sticks, chopped
600 ml (1 pint) water
bouquet garni
salt and pepper
1 × 439 g (15½ oz) can unsweetened chestnut purée
300 ml (½ pint) milk
1 teaspoon lemon juice
TO SERVE:
4 tablespoons smatana
1 tablespoon chopped parsley

Heat the oil in a pan, add the onion and fry until softened. Add the celery, water, bouquet garni, and salt and pepper to taste, cover and simmer gently for 20 minutes. Add the chestnut purée and milk and simmer for 10 minutes. Remove the bouquet garni.

Cool slightly, then place in an electric blender or food processor. Add the lemon juice and blend until smooth. Return to the pan to heat through. Pour into a warmed soup tureen and swirl the smatana on top. Sprinkle with the parsley to serve.
Serves 6

LENTIL AND CELERY SOUP

2 tablespoons oil
1 onion, chopped
3 celery sticks, chopped
1 clove garlic, crushed
175 g (6 oz) red lentils
1 litre (1¾ pints) water
bouquet garni
salt and pepper

Heat the oil in a large pan, add the onion and fry until softened. Add the remaining ingredients, with salt and pepper to taste. Bring to the boil, cover and simmer for 30 to 35 minutes, stirring occasionally.

Check the seasoning and remove the bouquet garni. Pour into a warmed soup tureen to serve.

Serves 6

MINESTRONE

2 tablespoons oil
2 onions, chopped
2 carrots, chopped
3 celery sticks, chopped
1 leek, sliced
2 cloves garlic, crushed
125 g (4 oz) green cabbage, shredded
bouquet garni
2.25 litres (4 pints) water
4 tablespoons tomato purée
4 tomatoes, skinned and chopped
2 tablespoons chopped parsley
25 g (1 oz) wholewheat pasta
salt and pepper
TO SERVE:
grated Parmesan cheese

Heat the oil in a large pan, add the onions and fry until softened. Add the carrots, celery, leek and garlic, cover and cook gently for 10 minutes. Add the remaining ingredients, with salt and pepper to taste, and bring to the boil. Cover and simmer gently for 30 to 40 minutes, until all the vegetables are tender. Remove the bouquet garni.

Pour into a warmed soup tureen and serve with grated Parmesan cheese.

Serves 8

BARLEY AND VEGETABLE BROTH

40 g (1½ oz) pot barley
2 tablespoons oil
1 large onion, chopped
2 celery sticks, thinly sliced
3 carrots, thinly sliced
2 cloves garlic, crushed
1 turnip, chopped
75 g (3 oz) French beans, cut into 2.5 cm (1 inch) lengths
bouquet garni
1.5 litres (2½ pints) water or vegetable stock
*1 tablespoon shoyu**
salt and pepper
4 tomatoes, skinned and chopped
2 tablespoons chopped parsley

Soak the barley in cold water to cover for 1 hour. Drain well and set aside.

Heat the oil in a pan, add the onion and fry until softened. Add the celery, carrots, garlic and turnip. Cover and cook gently for 10 minutes, shaking the pan occasionally.

Add the barley, French beans, bouquet garni, water or stock, shoyu, and salt and pepper to taste. Cover and simmer for 45 minutes, until tender.

Add the tomatoes and parsley and cook for a further 10 minutes. Check the seasoning and remove the bouquet garni. Pour into a warmed soup tureen to serve.

Serves 6 to 8

NOTE: Pot barley is the wholefood equivalent to pearl barley because it doesn't have the husk removed.

PEA SOUP

1 tablespoon oil
1 onion, chopped
1 clove garlic, crushed
2 celery sticks, chopped
250 g (8 oz) dried marrowfat peas, soaked overnight
1.5 litres (2½ pints) water
bouquet garni
salt and pepper
mint sprig to garnish

Heat the oil in a large pan, add the onion and cook until softened. Add the garlic and celery and cook for 5 minutes, stirring occasionally.

Drain the peas and add to the pan with the water, bouquet garni, and salt and pepper to taste. Cover and boil rapidly for 10 minutes, then simmer gently for 2 to 3 hours, until the peas are soft. Remove the bouquet garni.

Cool slightly, then place half the soup in an electric blender or food processor and work to a smooth purée. Return to the pan. Repeat with the remaining soup. Reheat the soup gently, adding a little more water if it is too thick. Pour into a warmed soup tureen and garnish with mint to serve.

Serves 4 to 6

BEAN SOUP

250 g (8 oz) haricot beans, soaked overnight
1.2 litres (2 pints) water
salt and pepper
2 tablespoons olive oil
1 large onion, chopped
2 celery sticks, sliced
2 cloves garlic, crushed
2 tablespoons chopped parsley

Drain the beans thoroughly, then place in a pan with the water. Cover, bring to the boil and boil rapidly for 10 minutes, then simmer for 1 to 1½ hours until soft, adding a little salt towards the end of cooking. Drain, reserving the cooking liquid.

Heat the oil in a large pan, add the onion, celery and garlic and fry for 5 minutes.

Place half the beans and 600 ml (1 pint) of the reserved liquid in an electric blender or food processor and work to a purée. Add to the onion and celery with remaining beans and bring to the boil. Add salt and pepper to taste and cook for 30 minutes.

Pour into a warmed soup tureen and sprinkle with the parsley to serve.
Serves 4 to 6

AVOCADO WITH RASPBERRY VINAIGRETTE

2 avocado pears, halved and stoned
1 tablespoon lemon juice
125 g (4 oz) raspberries
2 tablespoons olive oil
1 tablespoon wine vinegar
½ teaspoon clear honey
salt and pepper
fennel leaves to garnish (optional)

Peel each avocado half and place cut side down on a serving plate. Slice through the avocados lengthways, then separate the slices slightly. Brush lightly with the lemon juice.

Press the raspberries through a nylon sieve to remove the seeds, then mix with the oil, vinegar, honey and salt and pepper to taste. Spoon a little around each avocado pear and serve immediately, garnished with fennel.

Serves 4

STUFFED MUSHROOMS

500 g (1 lb) mushrooms
2 tablespoons oil
2 cloves garlic, crushed
1 tablespoon each chopped chives and parsley
1 egg yolk
2 tablespoons single cream
50 g (2 oz) wholewheat breadcrumbs
½ teaspoon chopped thyme
salt and pepper
SAUCE:
25 g (1 oz) margarine
25 g (1 oz) wholewheat flour
300 ml (½ pint) milk
50 g (2 oz) Cheddar cheese, grated
TO FINISH:
1 tablespoon grated Parmesan cheese
1 tablespoon wholewheat breadcrumbs, toasted
thyme sprigs to garnish

Remove the stalks from 16 of the mushrooms. Heat the oil in a frying pan, add the mushroom caps, rounded side down, and fry for 1 to 2 minutes to soften. Place rounded side down on 4 individual ovenproof dishes.

Chop the stalks and remaining mushrooms and mix with the remaining ingredients, seasoning with salt and pepper to taste. Place a spoonful in each mushroom cap.

To make the sauce, melt the margarine in a small pan and stir in the flour. Remove from the heat and stir in the milk until blended. Cook gently, stirring constantly, until thickened. Add salt and pepper to taste, then stir in the Cheddar cheese. Spoon over the mushrooms.

Mix the Parmesan cheese and breadcrumbs together, then sprinkle over the mushrooms. Cook in a preheated moderate oven, 180°C (350°F), Gas Mark 4, for 20 minutes, until golden. Serve immediately, garnished with thyme.

Serves 4

FALAFEL

250 g (8 oz) chick peas, soaked overnight
4 spring onions, chopped
2 cloves garlic, chopped
3 tablespoons water
4 large parsley sprigs
½ teaspoon ground cumin
1 teaspoon ground coriander
salt and pepper
oil for deep-frying

Drain the peas and place in an electric blender or food processor with the spring onions, garlic, water and parsley. Work to a purée, scraping down the sides when necessary. Stir in the remaining ingredients, with salt and pepper to taste, then turn into a bowl and leave for 1 to 2 hours and dry out slightly.

Form the mixture into walnut-sized balls and flatten slightly. Heat the oil in a deep-fryer, add the falafel and fry for about 4 minutes, until golden. Drain on kitchen paper.

Serve hot with Piquante Sauce (see page 93).

Serves 6

BABA GHANOUSH

This is a popular dish in the Middle East where it is served quite often. If possible, grill the aubergines over charcoal as this gives them a delicious smoky flavour that blends well with tahini.

2 large aubergines
2 cloves garlic, crushed
4 tablespoons tahini (see below)*
juice of 1 lemon
½ teaspoon ground cumin
2 tablespoons chopped parsley
salt and pepper
TO GARNISH:
2 black olives, halved and stoned

Prick the aubergines all over with a fork, cut in half and place, cut side down, on a grill pan rack. Place under a preheated low grill until the skins are black and start to blister and the flesh feels soft. Peel and wash the aubergines and squeeze out as much of the juice as possible, as this is rather bitter.

Chop the aubergine flesh, place in an electric blender or food processor with the garlic and blend to a purée. Add the tahini and lemon juice alternately, blending between each addition. Turn into a bowl and stir in the cumin, parsley, and salt and pepper to taste.

Turn into a shallow serving dish and garnish with the olives. Serve with wholewheat pitta bread.

Serves 6

NOTE: Tahini is a sesame seed paste. It is available from healthfood stores and delicatessens.

ARTICHOKE WITH HERB MAYONNAISE

4 globe artichokes
salt
5 tablespoons Green Herb Dressing (see page 92)
4 tablespoons fromage frais

Trim the points of the artichoke leaves square with scissors and cut off the stalk to level the base.

Place in a large pan of boiling salted water and cook for 35 to 45 minutes, until one of the leaves can be pulled out easily. Place upside down in a collander to drain and cool.

Gently ease the outer leaves so that you can remove the centre purple-tinged leaves and the 'choke', which is inedible; take care not to remove any of the 'fond' underneath.

Fold the dressing into the fromage frais and spoon a tablespoon into the bottom of each artichoke. Place on individual dishes and serve the remaining herb sauce separately.
Serves 4

PEANUT DIP WITH CRUDITÉS

2 tablespoons sunflower oil
1 onion, finely chopped
2 cloves garlic, crushed
½ teaspoon chilli powder
1 teaspoon ground cumin
1 teaspoon ground coriander
6 tablespoons crunchy peanut butter
120 ml (4 fl oz) water
*1 teaspoon shoyu**
1 teaspoon lemon juice
CRUDITÉS:
1 small cauliflower
1 bunch of radishes
1 red pepper, cored and seeded
6 celery sticks
6 carrots

Heat the oil in a pan, add the onion and fry until softened. Add the garlic and spices, stir and cook for 1 minute. Mix in the peanut butter, then gradually blend in the water, stirring until thickened. Add the shoyu and lemon juice and leave to cool.

Break the cauliflower into florets and halve the radishes if large. Cut the remaining vegetables into long thin pieces.

Turn the dip into a dish, place on a large plate and surround with the vegetables.

Serves 6

HUMMOUS

250 g (8 oz) chick peas, soaked overnight
*150 ml (¼ pint) tahini**
3 cloves garlic
juice of 1-2 lemons
salt and pepper
TO FINISH:
1 tablespoon olive oil blended with 1 teaspoon paprika
1 teaspoon chopped parsley

Drain the chick peas, place in a pan and cover with cold water. Bring to the boil, cover and boil rapidly for 10 minutes, then simmer gently for 1½ to 2 hours, until soft; the time will vary depending on the age and quality of the peas. Drain, reserving 300 ml (½ pint) of the liquid.

Place the chick peas in an electric blender or food processor and add the remaining ingredients, seasoning with salt and pepper to taste, and enough of the reserved liquid to blend to a soft creamy paste.

Turn into a shallow serving dish, dribble over the blended oil and sprinkle with the parsley. Serve with pitta bread.

Serves 8 to 10

NOTE: This will keep for up to 1 week, covered in the refrigerator.

FLAGEOLET VINAIGRETTE

250 g (8 oz) flageolet beans, soaked overnight
salt
6 tablespoons French Dressing (see page 92)
1 red pepper, cored, seeded and chopped
4 spring onions, chopped
1 tablespoon chopped mixed herbs: parsley, thyme and mint
2 celery sticks, thinly sliced

Drain the beans, place in a pan and cover with cold water. Bring to the boil and boil rapidly for 10 minutes. Cover and simmer for about 1 hour, until tender, adding a little salt towards the end of cooking. Drain thoroughly and place in a bowl.

Pour over the dressing while still warm and mix well. Leave to cool, then add the remaining ingredients. Toss thoroughly and transfer to a shallow dish to serve.

Serves 4

TZATSIKI

500 g (1 lb) natural yogurt (preferably Greek)
1 cucumber, peeled and grated
3 cloves garlic, crushed
salt and pepper
1 tablespoon chopped mint

Mix the yogurt with a fork until smooth. Drain the cucumber, then add to the yogurt with the garlic, and salt and pepper to taste. Chill for 2 hours, then turn into a serving bowl and sprinkle with the mint. Serve with wholewheat pitta bread.

Serves 6

SALADS

CASHEW COLESLAW

250 g (8 oz) firm white cabbage, shredded
3 celery sticks, sliced
3 red-skinned dessert apples, cored and thinly sliced
4 spring onions, sliced
50 g (2 oz) cashew nuts, toasted
2 tablespoons chopped parsley
150 ml (1/4 pint) mayonnaise
2 tablespoons natural yogurt

Place the cabbage, celery, apples, spring onions, cashews and parsley in a mixing bowl.

Mix the mayonnaise and yogurt together, then pour over the salad and toss thoroughly. Transfer to a salad bowl to serve.

Serves 6 to 8

RED BEAN AND BEANSHOOT SALAD

175 g (6 oz) red kidney beans, soaked overnight
salt
125 g (4 oz) mushrooms, sliced
6 tablespoons Vinaigrette Dressing (see page 92)
250 g (8 oz) beanshoots
1 red pepper, cored, seeded and thinly sliced
2 tablespoons toasted sunflower seeds
2 tablespoons chopped parsley

Drain the beans, place in a pan and cover with cold water. Bring to the boil, cover and boil rapidly for 10 minutes, then simmer for 45 minutes to 1 hour, until tender; add a little salt towards the end of cooking.

Drain the beans and place in a bowl with the mushrooms. Pour over the dressing and mix thoroughly. Leave to cool.

Add the remaining ingredients and toss well. Transfer to a shallow dish to serve.

Serves 6

CELERIAC AND EGG SALAD

500 g (1 lb) celeriac
6 tablespoons Vinaigrette Dressing (see page 92)
2 hard-boiled eggs
1 tablespoon chopped parsley

Grate the celeriac finely and place in a mixing bowl. Pour over the dressing, toss thoroughly and leave for 1 hour.

Shred the egg whites finely and mix with the celeriac. Place in a shallow serving dish and sieve the egg yolks over the top. Sprinkle with the parsley to serve.

Serves 4

CHICORY AND SESAME SALAD

3 heads of chicory
2 oranges
1 bunch of watercress
25 g (1 oz) sesame seeds, toasted
4 tablespoons olive oil
1 tablespoon lemon juice
salt and pepper

Cut the chicory diagonally into 1 cm (½ inch) slices and place in a bowl. Remove the peel and pith from the oranges and cut the flesh into segments, holding the fruit over the bowl so that any juice is included.

Divide the watercress into sprigs and add to the bowl with the sesame seeds.

Whisk together the oil, lemon juice, and salt and pepper to taste, then pour over the salad and toss thoroughly. Transfer to a salad bowl to serve.

Serves 4 to 6

CAULIFLOWER AND CRESS SALAD

500 g (1 lb) cauliflower, broken into florets
salt
1 carton mustard and cress, trimmed
25 g (1 oz) pumpkin seeds
4 tablespoons French Dressing (see page 92)

Cook the cauliflower in boiling salted water for 1 minute; drain and leave to cool completely. Place in a bowl with the remaining ingredients and toss thoroughly. Transfer to a shallow dish to serve.

Serves 4

NOTE: Pumpkin seeds are available from healthfood stores.

SPRING GREEN AND PEPPER SALAD

250 g (8 oz) spring greens, very finely shredded
4 tablespoons Shoyu Dressing (see page 92)
3 celery sticks, sliced
4 spring onions, chopped
1 red pepper, cored, seeded and diced

Place the spring greens in a bowl with the dressing, toss thoroughly and leave to marinate for 1 hour. Add the remaining ingredients and toss thoroughly. Transfer to a salad bowl to serve.

Serves 4 to 6

ARTICHOKE VINAIGRETTE

500 g (1 lb) Jerusalem artichokes, scrubbed
4 tablespoons French Dressing (see page 92)
1 tablespoon chopped parsley
1 tablespoon pumpkin seeds
1 teaspoon lemon juice

Grate the artichokes coarsely and place in a mixing bowl with the remaining ingredients. Toss thoroughly and leave for 1 hour. Transfer to a shallow serving dish to serve.

Serves 4 to 6

NOTE: Pumpkin seeds are available from healthfood stores.

TOMATO AND YOGURT SALAD

A delicious refreshing salad accompaniment to serve in the summer – perfect for 'al fresco' meals.

300 g (10 oz) natural yogurt
2 tablespoons chopped basil
salt and pepper
500 g (1 lb) tomatoes, skinned and cut into wedges

Place the yogurt in a bowl, add the chopped basil, and salt and pepper to taste and mix well. Stir in the tomatoes, then transfer to a shallow serving dish.

Chill in the refrigerator for about 30 minutes before serving.

Serves 4 to 6

Variation: If basil is unobtainable, replace it with 1 tablespoon chopped fresh coriander leaves. This salad makes an excellent accompaniment to serve with curries and other hot spicy dishes.

TABBOULEH

75 g (3 oz) bulgur wheat
1 teacup chopped parsley
3 tablespoons chopped mint
4 spring onions, chopped
½ cucumber, finely diced
2 tablespoons olive oil
juice of 1 lemon
salt and pepper

Soak the bulgar wheat in cold water for 1 hour. Line a sieve with muslin and tip the wheat into it. Lift out the muslin and squeeze out as much moisture as possible.

Place the wheat in a bowl and add the remaining ingredients, seasoning with salt and pepper to taste. Toss thoroughly, then transfer to a shallow dish to serve.

Serves 4

NOTE: Bulgur wheat is available from healthfood stores.

ADUKI BEAN SALAD

250 g (8 oz) aduki beans, soaked overnight
salt and pepper
6 tablespoons Ginger Dressing (see page 92)
6 spring onions, chopped
4 tomatoes, skinned and chopped
3 celery sticks, sliced
2 tablespoons chopped parsley

Drain the beans, place in a pan of boiling salted water and boil rapidly for 10 minutes. Cover and cook for 30 to 35 minutes or until tender. Drain well and mix with the dressing while still warm. Leave to cool.

Add the remaining ingredients, seasoning with salt and pepper to taste. Mix thoroughly and transfer to a shallow dish to serve.

Serves 6

NOTE: Aduki beans are a small type of red kidney bean. If unobtainable, use kidney beans instead.

BUCKWHEAT AND CORN SALAD

*75 g (3 oz) toasted buckwheat**
salt
4 tablespoons Ginger Dressing (see page 92)
1 × 198 g (7 oz) can sweetcorn, drained
1 green pepper, cored, seeded and chopped
3 tomatoes, skinned and chopped
2 tablespoons chopped parsley
25 g (1 oz) toasted sunflower seeds

Place the buckwheat in a pan of boiling salted water, cover and simmer gently for 15 minutes. Drain thoroughly and place in a bowl with the dressing.

Add the remaining ingredients and toss thoroughly. Transfer to a shallow dish to serve.

Serves 4

NOTE: Buckwheat is available from healthfood stores.

POTATO AND EGG MAYONNAISE

500 g (1 lb) waxy (salad) potatoes
salt
2 tablespoons French Dressing (see page 92)
4 spring onions, sliced
4 hard-boiled eggs, chopped
2 dill pickles, chopped
3 tablespoons mayonnaise
3 tablespoons natural yogurt
1 tablespoon chopped fennel to garnish

Cook the potatoes in their skins in boiling salted water until tender. Drain well, chop roughly and place in a bowl. Pour over the dressing while still warm, toss thoroughly and leave to cool. Add the spring onions, eggs and dill pickles.

Mix together the mayonnaise, yogurt and 2 tablespoons juice from the dill pickles until smooth. Pour over the salad and mix thoroughly. Transfer to a shallow dish and sprinkle with the fennel to serve.

Serves 4

Swedish Potato Salad: Omit the hard-boiled eggs. Substitute with 125 g (4 oz) chopped cooked beetroot.

POTATO AND MINT VINAIGRETTE

500 g (1 lb) new potatoes
salt
3 tablespoons French Dressing (see page 92)
3 tablespoons chopped mint
1 bunch radishes, thinly sliced

Cook the potatoes in their skins in boiling salted water until tender. Drain well and mix with the dressing while still warm, then leave to cool.

Add the chopped mint and radishes and mix well. Transfer to a salad bowl to serve.

Serves 4

Potato and Onion Vinaigrette: Omit the mint and radishes from the above recipe. Substitute with 6 chopped spring onions.

BROWN RICE AND HAZELNUT SALAD

175 g (6 oz) brown rice
salt
75 g (3 oz) hazelnuts, chopped and toasted
1 red pepper, cored, seeded and diced
6 spring onions, finely sliced
3 celery sticks, chopped
50 g (2 oz) button mushrooms, sliced
6 tablespoons French Dressing (see page 92)
3 tablespoons chopped parsley

Cook the rice in boiling salted water for 30 to 40 minutes, until tender. Rinse and drain well.

Place in a bowl with the remaining ingredients and toss thoroughly. Transfer to a shallow dish to serve.

Serves 6 to 8

BULGUR WHEAT VINAIGRETTE

75 g (3 oz) bulgur wheat
4 tomatoes, skinned and chopped
50 g (2 oz) black olives, halved and stoned
1 celery stick, thinly sliced
4 spring onions, chopped
2 tablespoons chopped parsley
2 tablespoons toasted sunflower seeds
3 tablespoons French Dressing (see page 92)

Soak the bulgur wheat in cold water for 1 hour. Line a sieve with muslin and tip the wheat into it. Lift out the muslin and squeeze out as much moisture as possible.

Place the wheat in a bowl, add the remaining ingredients and mix well. Transfer to a shallow dish to serve.

Serves 4

NOTE: Bulgur wheat is available from healthfood stores.

WHOLEWHEAT SALAD

250 g (8 oz) wheat, soaked overnight
salt
6 tablespoons Shoyu Dressing (see page 92)
1 red pepper, cored, seeded and chopped
50 g (2 oz) raisins
2 celery sticks, diced
2 tablespoons chopped parsley

Drain the wheat thoroughly. Place in a pan, cover with lightly salted water, bring to the boil and simmer for 1 to 1½ hours; drain well. Mix with the dressing while still warm, then leave to cool.

Add the remaining ingredients, toss well, then transfer to a shallow dish to serve.

Serves 4 to 6

VEGETABLE DISHES

VEGETABLE RISOTTO

4 tablespoons oil
1 onion, chopped
175 g (6 oz) brown rice
3 cloves garlic, crushed
600 ml (1 pint) water
1 teaspoon salt
2 celery sticks, thinly sliced
1 red pepper, cored, seeded and diced
250 g (8 oz) button mushrooms, sliced
1 × 425 g (15 oz) can red kidney beans, drained
3 tablespoons chopped parsley
*1 tablespoon shoyu**
50 g (2 oz) roasted cashew nuts
chopped parsley to garnish

Heat 2 tablespoons of the oil in a pan, add the onion and fry until softened. Add the rice and 2 cloves garlic and cook, stirring, for 2 minutes. Add the water and salt and bring to the boil, stirring. Cover and simmer gently for 35 to 40 minutes, until all the water has been absorbed.

Heat the remaining oil in a frying pan, add the celery and red pepper and fry for 5 minutes, until softened. Add the mushrooms and remaining garlic and fry for 3 minutes.

Add the cooked rice, kidney beans, parsley, shoyu and nuts. Cook, stirring to mix, until the beans are heated through. Serve garnished with parsley, and accompanied by a green salad.

Serves 4

TIAN

This is a Provençale family dish which takes its name from the heavy earthenware dish in which it is cooked.

3 tablespoons olive oil
1 onion, chopped
2 cloves garlic, crushed
500 g (1 lb) courgettes, chopped
250 g (8 oz) spinach, cooked, drained and chopped
4 tablespoons brown rice, cooked
3 eggs, beaten
50 g (2 oz) Gruyère cheese, grated
salt and pepper
1 tablespoon fresh wholewheat breadcrumbs
1 tablespoon grated Parmesan cheese

Heat the oil in a frying pan, add the onion and cook until softened. Add the garlic and courgettes and cook for 5 minutes, stirring occasionally. Stir in the spinach, rice, eggs, Gruyère cheese, and salt and pepper to taste and mix well.

Turn into a greased 1.2 litre (2 pint) earthenware gratin dish and sprinkle with the breadcrumbs and Parmesan cheese.

Bake in a preheated moderate oven, 180°C (350°F), Gas Mark 4, for 35 minutes, until golden.

Serve with salad and wholewheat bread.

Serves 4

STIR-FRIED VEGETABLES WITH TOFU

*3 tablespoons shoyu**
3 tablespoons dry sherry
1 cm (½ inch) piece root ginger, peeled and finely chopped
2 cloves garlic, crushed
*250 g (8 oz) firm tofu**
about 2 tablespoons sesame oil
1 large onion, sliced
175 g (6 oz) mangetouts, topped, tailed and halved
1 red pepper, cored, seeded and sliced
175 g (6 oz) button mushrooms, sliced
500 g (1 lb) beanshoots
2 tablespoons sesame seeds, toasted

Mix the shoyu, sherry, chopped ginger and garlic together in a bowl. Cut the tofu into cubes and add to the bowl, stirring to coat completely. Leave to marinate for 1 hour, then drain, reserving the marinade.

Heat the oil in a large wok, add the tofu cubes and stir-fry for about 2 minutes, until beginning to brown on all sides. Remove with a slotted spoon and keep warm.

Reheat the oil, adding a little more if necessary. Add the onion and stir-fry for 2 minutes. Add the mangetouts and red pepper and stir-fry for 2 minutes. Add the mushrooms, beanshoots and reserved marinade and stir-fry for 2 minutes, until heated through.

Lightly stir in the tofu, then turn onto a warmed serving dish. Sprinkle with the sesame seeds to serve.

Serves 4

VEGETABLE CRUMBLE

1 cauliflower, broken into florets
salt
2 tablespoons oil
4 tablespoons wholewheat flour
350 ml (12 fl oz) milk
1 × 326 g (11½ oz) can sweetcorn, drained
2 tablespoons chopped parsley
125 g (4 oz) matured Cheddar cheese, grated

TOPPING:
50 g (2 oz) wholewheat flour
25 g (1 oz) margarine
25 g (1 oz) porridge oats
25 g (1 oz) chopped almonds

Cook the cauliflower in boiling salted water for 5 minutes. Drain, reserving the water.

Heat the oil in the same pan and stir in the flour. Remove from the heat, add the milk, stirring until blended. Add 150 ml (¼ pint) of the reserved cooking liquid, bring to the boil and cook for 3 minutes, until thickened. Stir in the sweetcorn, parsley and half the cheese. Gently fold in the cauliflower and turn into a 1.5 litre (3 pint) ovenproof dish.

For the topping, place the flour in a bowl and rub in the margarine until the mixture resembles fine breadcrumbs. Add the oats, almonds and remaining cheese. Sprinkle over the vegetable mixture and bake in a preheated moderately hot oven, 190°C (375°F), Gas Mark 5, for 30 minutes, until golden brown and crisp.

Serves 4

SPINACH LATTICE FLAN

2 tablespoons oil
1 large onion, chopped
2 cloves garlic, crushed
500 g (1 lb) frozen chopped spinach, thawed and drained
2 eggs
½ teaspoon ground nutmeg
250 g (8 oz) Ricotta or curd cheese
50 g (2 oz) Parmesan cheese, grated
salt and pepper
WHOLEWHEAT SHORTCRUST PASTRY:
250 g (8 oz) wholewheat flour
125 g (4 oz) plain flour
175 g (6 oz) margarine
3-4 tablespoons iced water
beaten egg to glaze

Heat the oil in a pan and fry the onion until softened. Add the garlic and spinach and cook gently for 10 minutes, stirring occasionally. Cool slightly then beat in the eggs, nutmeg, cheeses, and salt and pepper to taste.

To make the pastry, place the flours in a mixing bowl and rub in the margarine until the mixture resembles breadcrumbs. Add enough water to mix to a firm dough, then turn onto a floured surface and knead lightly until smooth. Cut off two thirds of the pastry, roll out thinly and use to line a 23 cm (9 inch) flan dish, leaving it overlapping the side.

Spread the filling evenly in the pastry case. Moisten pastry edge. Roll out remaining pastry and cut into 5 mm (¼ inch) strips. Arrange in a lattice design over the filling and press the edges to secure. Brush with egg and bake in a preheated moderately hot oven, 200°C (400°F), Gas Mark 6, for 45 to 50 minutes, until golden. Serve warm or cold with a crisp mixed salad.

Serves 6

PROVENÇALE PANCAKES

PANCAKE BATTER:
*50 g (2 oz) buckwheat flour**
50 g (2 oz) plain flour
pinch of salt
1 egg, beaten
300 ml (½ pint) milk
1 tablespoon oil
FILLING:
2 tablespoons olive oil
1 onion, chopped
2 cloves garlic, crushed
1 green or red pepper, cored, seeded and chopped
1 small aubergine, chopped
4 large tomatoes, skinned and chopped
1 tablespoon tomato purée
salt and pepper to taste
TO FINISH:
25 g (1 oz) margarine, melted
2 tablespoons grated Parmesan cheese

Place the flours and salt in a bowl and make a well in the centre. Add the egg, then gradually stir in half the milk and the oil. Beat thoroughly until smooth. Add the remaining milk.

Heat a 15 cm (6 inch) omelet pan and add a few drops of oil. Pour in 1 tablespoon of the batter, lifting the pan to coat the bottom evenly. Cook until the underside is brown, then turn over and cook for 10 seconds. Turn onto a warmed plate. Repeat with the remaining batter, making 12 pancakes. Stack interleaved with greaseproof paper.

For the filling, heat the oil in a pan and cook the onion until softened. Add the garlic, pepper and aubergine and fry for 10 minutes, stirring occasionally. Add remaining ingredients, cover and cook for 15 minutes.

Divide filling between pancakes, roll up and place in an oiled shallow ovenproof dish. Top with the margarine and cheese. Bake in a preheated moderately hot oven, 190°C (375°F), Gas Mark 5, for 15 minutes. Serve immediately.
Serves 4

SPINACH AND POTATO PATTIES

1 tablespoon oil
1 onion, chopped
1 clove garlic, crushed
250 g (8 oz) frozen chopped spinach, thawed and drained
500 g (1 lb) potatoes, boiled and mashed
¼ teaspoon ground nutmeg
125 g (4 oz) Cheddar cheese, grated
salt and pepper
wholewheat flour for coating
oil for shallow-frying

Heat the oil in a pan, add the onion and garlic and fry until softened. Squeeze the spinach dry and add to the pan with the potato, nutmeg, cheese, and salt and pepper to taste; mix thoroughly. Shape the mixture into 8 balls, using dampened hands, and flatten slightly.

Place some flour in a polythene bag, add the patties one at a time and shake to coat completely.

Fry in hot shallow oil for 2 minutes on each side, until golden brown.

Serve with salad and crusty bread.

Serves 3 to 4

STUFFED SPINACH LEAVES

12 large spinach leaves, stalks removed
salt and pepper
1 tablespoon oil
1 onion, chopped
2 cloves garlic, crushed
250 g (8 oz) mushrooms, chopped
75 g (3 oz) wholewheat breadcrumbs
1 tablespoon chopped mixed herbs, e.g. parsley, thyme and marjoram
1 egg, beaten
SAUCE:
2 egg yolks
1 tablespoon lemon juice

Put the spinach in a large pan with 300 ml (½ pint) salted water and boil for 2 minutes. Drain, reserving the liquid. Rinse under cold water, then place on kitchen paper and pat dry.

Heat the oil in a pan, add the onion and fry until softened. Add garlic and mushrooms and cook for 5 minutes. Stir in the breadcrumbs, herbs, egg, and salt and pepper to taste.

Place 1 tablespoon of the mixture in the centre of each spinach leaf, fold in both sides and roll up carefully.

Lay the spinach rolls in a shallow ovenproof dish and pour over 150 ml (¼ pint) of the reserved liquid. Cover with foil and bake in a preheated moderately hot oven, 190°C (375°F), Gas Mark 5, for 45 minutes. Strain and reserve juices; keep rolls warm.

For the sauce, whisk the egg yolks with the lemon juice in a heatproof bowl over a pan of simmering water. Add reserved cooking juices and stir for about 5 minutes, until thickened. Season with salt and pepper and pour over the spinach rolls. Serve as an accompaniment or starter.

Serves 4

MUSHROOM GOUGÈRE

CHOUX PASTRY:
50 g (2 oz) margarine
150 ml (¼ pint) water
65 g (2½ oz) wholewheat flour
2 eggs
50 g (2 oz) Cheddar cheese, grated

FILLING:
2 tablespoons oil
1 onion, chopped
250 g (8 oz) mushrooms, sliced
2 cloves garlic, crushed
1 tablespoon wholewheat flour
150 ml (¼ pint) vegetable stock
75 g (3 oz) walnuts, roughly chopped
2 tablespoons chopped parsley
salt and pepper

Melt the margarine in a large pan, add the water and bring to the boil. Add the flour all at once and beat until the mixture leaves the side of the pan. Cool slightly, then add the eggs one at a time, beating vigorously until glossy. Beat in the cheese. Spoon the pastry around the edge of a greased 1.2 litre (2 pint) ovenproof dish.

To make the filling, heat the oil in a pan, add the onion and fry until softened. Add the mushrooms and garlic and fry for 2 minutes. Stir in the flour, then add the stock and bring to the boil, stirring. Cook for 3 minutes, until thickened. Stir in all but 2 tablespoons of the walnuts, the parsley, and salt and pepper to taste.

Pour the filling into the centre of the dish and sprinkle with the reserved walnuts.

Bake in a preheated moderately hot oven, 200°C (400°F), Gas Mark 6, for 40 to 45 minutes, until the pastry is golden brown. Serve immediately.
Serves 4

AUBERGINE GALETTE

2 large aubergines
salt and pepper
150 ml (¼ pint) olive oil
1 onion, chopped
1 clove garlic, crushed
500 g (1 lb) tomatoes, skinned and chopped
1 egg
250 g (8 oz) Ricotta or curd cheese
1 tablespoon sesame seeds, toasted

Slice the aubergines, sprinkle with salt and leave in a colander for 1 hour. Rinse well and dry on kitchen paper.

Heat 2 tablespoons oil in a pan, add the onion and fry until softened. Add the garlic and tomatoes and simmer, uncovered, for 5 to 7 minutes.

Mix the egg with the cheese, adding salt and pepper to taste.

Heat the remaining oil in a frying pan, add the aubergines and cook on both sides until golden. Drain on kitchen paper.

Arrange a layer of overlapping aubergine slices on the bottom and side of an 18 cm (7 inch) springform cake tin. Cover with half the tomato mixture, then top with half the cheese mixture. Repeat the layers, finishing with aubergine. Cover with foil and bake in a preheated moderate oven, 180°C (350°F), Gas Mark 4, for 40 to 50 minutes.

Turn out onto a warmed serving dish and sprinkle with the sesame seeds. Cut into wedges and serve with crusty wholewheat bread.

Serves 4

CURRIED VEGBURGERS

2 tablespoons oil
2 onions, chopped
1 clove garlic, crushed
2 carrots, chopped
2 celery sticks, chopped
2 teaspoons curry powder
2 tablespoons chopped parsley
500 g (1 lb) potatoes, boiled and mashed
salt and pepper
wholewheat breadcrumbs for coating
oil for shallow-frying

Heat the oil in a pan, add the onions and fry until softened. Add the garlic, carrots and celery and fry for 5 minutes, stirring. Mix in the curry powder and cook for 1 minute.

Add the fried vegetables and parsley to the potato and season with salt and pepper to taste. Divide the mixture into 8 pieces, shape into rounds, and coat with breadcrumbs. Press to flatten slightly and fry for 2 minutes on each side until golden. Serve with Piquant Sauce (page 93).

Serves 4

SPINACH AND MUSHROOM PLAIT

3 tablespoons oil
1 onion, chopped
500 g (1 lb) frozen chopped spinach, half-thawed
pinch of grated nutmeg
salt and pepper
250 g (8 oz) button mushrooms, sliced
2 cloves garlic, crushed
wholewheat shortcrust pastry, made with 350 g (12 oz) flour (see Spinach Lattice Flan, page 42)
beaten egg to glaze
1 tablespoon sesame seeds

Heat 1 tablespoon oil in a pan, add the onion and fry until softened. Add the spinach, nutmeg, and salt and pepper to taste and cook for 5 minutes, stirring. Turn onto a plate to cool.

Wipe out the pan and heat the remaining oil. Add the mushrooms and garlic and fry until softened. Season to taste with salt and pepper; allow to cool.

Roll out the pastry on a floured surface to 30×35 cm (12×14 inches). Mark into 3 sections lengthways. Moisten the edges with water. Make diagonal slits along the outer sections of the pastry, 2.5 cm (1 inch) apart and 7.5 cm (3 inches) long.

Spread half the spinach mixture over the centre section of the dough, place the mushrooms on top, then cover with remaining spinach. Fold the cut pastry strips over the spinach to give a plaited effect. Press each end firmly to seal. Carefully lift onto a baking sheet and chill for 20 minutes.

Brush with egg and sprinkle with sesame seeds. Bake in a preheated moderately hot oven, 200°C (400°F), Gas Mark 6, for 30 to 35 minutes, until golden brown. Serve with salad.

Serves 4 to 6

WALNUT-STUFFED AUBERGINES

2 large aubergines
2 tablespoons olive oil
1 large onion, chopped
2 cloves garlic, crushed
3 celery sticks, chopped
175 g (6 oz) mushrooms, chopped
6 tablespoons brown rice, cooked
50 g (2 oz) walnuts, ground
1 tablespoon tomato purée
2 tablespoons chopped parsley
salt and pepper to taste
75 g (3 oz) Cheddar cheese, grated

Prick the aubergines all over, cut in half and place cut side down on a greased baking sheet. Bake in a preheated moderately hot oven, 190°C (375°F), Gas Mark 5, for 30 minutes.

Meanwhile, heat the oil in a pan, add the onion and fry until softened. Add the garlic and celery and fry for 5 minutes. Add the mushrooms and cook, stirring, for 3 minutes. Stir in rice, walnuts, tomato purée, parsley, and seasoning. Turn off the heat.

Scoop the flesh from the aubergines, without breaking the skins, chop finely and mix with the fried mixture. Pile into the aubergine skins, sprinkle with the cheese and place under a preheated hot grill until heated through. Serve immediately.
Serves 4

VEGETABLE CURRY

2 tablespoons oil
1 onion, sliced
2 teaspoons ground coriander
2 teaspoons ground cumin
2 cloves garlic, crushed
2 tablespoons finely chopped root ginger
1 × 397 g (14 oz) can chopped tomatoes
150 ml (1/4 pint) water
1 green chilli, finely chopped
2 potatoes, diced
2 carrots, sliced
175 g (6 oz) okra, topped, tailed and cut into 2.5 cm (1 inch) lengths
250 g (8 oz) cauliflower, broken into florets
salt and pepper
2 tablespoons chopped fresh coriander

ACCOMPANIMENTS:

4 poppadums

DAHL:

2 tablespoons oil
1 onion, chopped
2 cloves garlic, chopped
2 teaspoons garam masala
1 teaspoon turmeric
175 g (6 oz) red lentils
600 ml (1 pint) water
1 tablespoon chopped coriander

CUCUMBER RAITA:

1/4 cucumber
150 g (5 oz) natural yogurt
paprika

ONION RELISH:

125 g (4 oz) Spanish onion, thinly sliced
1 tablespoon lemon juice
1/4 teaspoon paprika
pinch of cayenne pepper

Heat the oil in a large pan, add the onion and fry until softened. Add the ground coriander, cumin, garlic and ginger and fry for 1 minute, stirring constantly. Add the tomatoes, water, chilli, potatoes, carrots, okra, cauliflower and salt and pepper to taste. Mix to coat the vegetables with the sauce. Cover and cook gently for 20 minutes, until tender. Stir in the chopped coriander.

Serve on a bed of brown rice with the following accompaniments.

POPPADUMS

Fry in a deep hot oil for a few seconds until they have puffed up. Drain thoroughly on kitchen paper.

DAHL

Heat the oil in a pan, add the onion and fry until softened. Add the garlic and spices and fry for 1 minute. Add the remaining ingredients, bring to the boil and simmer for 20 minutes, stirring occasionally. Serve hot.

CUCUMBER RAITA

Grate the cucumber and drain off any juices. Mix with the yogurt, and salt to taste. Turn into a serving bowl and sprinkle with paprika.

ONION RELISH

Mix the onion with the lemon juice, peppers and salt to taste until well coated. Leave to stand for 1 hour, then turn into a serving dish and sprinkle with more paprika.

Serves 4

CHEESE AND EGG DISHES

SPINACH AND CHEESE SOUFFLÉ

25 g (1 oz) margarine
25 g (1 oz) wholewheat flour
150 ml (¼ pint) milk
3 eggs, separated
125 g (4 oz) frozen spinach purée, thawed
50 g (2 oz) Cheddar cheese, grated
¼ teaspoon grated nutmeg
salt and pepper
2 tablespoons grated Parmesan cheese

Tie a double band of foil around a greased 1.2 litre (2 pint) soufflé dish, to come 5 cm (2 inches) above the rim.

Melt the margarine in a pan and stir in the flour. Remove from the heat and stir in the milk. Return to the heat and slowly bring to the boil, stirring. Cook for 3 minutes, then add the egg yolks, spinach, Cheddar cheese, nutmeg, and salt and pepper to taste. Mix thoroughly.

Whisk the egg whites until fairly stiff, then carefully fold into the spinach mixture using a metal spoon.

Turn into the prepared dish, sprinkle with the Parmesan cheese and cook in a preheated moderately hot oven, 190°C (375°F), Gas Mark 5, for 30 to 35 minutes, until risen and golden. Serve immediately.
Serves 4

CHEESE AND VEGETABLE GRATIN

2 tablespoons oil
2 onions, sliced
1 clove garlic, crushed
350 g (12 oz) courgettes, sliced
1 tablespoon chopped parsley
1 teaspoon chopped thyme
salt and pepper
4 large tomatoes, skinned and sliced
25 g (1 oz) margarine
25 g (1 oz) wholewheat flour
300 ml (½ pint) milk
125 g (4 oz) Cheddar cheese, grated
1 tablespoon fresh wholewheat breadcrumbs

Heat the oil in a pan, add the onions and fry gently until softened. Add the garlic, courgettes, herbs, and salt and pepper to taste, and cook for 5 minutes, stirring occasionally.

Put half the mixture in a 1.5 litre (2½ pint) pie dish and cover with the tomatoes. Top with remaining mixture.

Melt the margarine in a saucepan, stir in the flour, remove from the heat and blend in the milk. Bring to the boil, stirring constantly, until the sauce thickens. Add half of the cheese, and salt and pepper to taste and pour over the courgettes.

Sprinkle with the breadcrumbs, then the remaining cheese. Bake in a preheated moderate oven, 180°C (350°F), Gas Mark 4, for 30 minutes, until golden.

Serves 4

BROCCOLI AND CHEESE FLAN

CHEESE PASTRY:
125 g (4 oz) wholewheat flour
50 g (2 oz) plain flour, sifted
75 g (3 oz) margarine
50 g (2 oz) matured Cheddar cheese, grated
½ teaspoon dried mixed herbs
1 egg yolk
iced water to mix

FILLING:
250 g (8 oz) broccoli
2 eggs, beaten
150 ml (¼ pint) milk
125 g (4 oz) Cheddar cheese, grated
1 teaspoon dry mustard
salt and pepper

Place the flours in a bowl and rub in the margarine until the mixture resembles fine breadcrumbs. Stir in the cheese and herbs. Make a well in the centre and add the egg yolk and enough water to mix to a firm dough.

Turn onto a floured surface and knead lightly until smooth. Roll out and use to line a 20 cm (8 inch) flan dish. Prick the base with a fork; chill for 20 minutes. Bake 'blind' in a preheated moderately hot oven, 200°C (400°F), Gas Mark 6, for 10 minutes. Remove the foil and beans, return to oven for 5 minutes.

Meanwhile, cook the broccoli in boiling salted water for 5 to 6 minutes. Rinse in cold water, drain thoroughly, then chop roughly.

Mix the beaten eggs with the milk, three quarters of the cheese, the mustard, and salt and pepper to taste.

Arrange the broccoli in the flan case and pour over the egg mixture. Sprinkle with remaining cheese and return to the oven for 35 minutes, until set and golden.

Serves 4

RICOTTA AND SPINACH PANCAKES

PANCAKE BATTER:
125 g (4 oz) wholewheat flour
pinch of salt
1 egg, beaten
300 ml (½ pint) milk
FILLING:
350 g (12 oz) frozen chopped spinach, half thawed
175 g (6 oz) Ricotta or curd cheese
2 tablespoons grated Parmesan cheese
1 egg
salt and pepper
grated nutmeg
SAUCE:
2 tablespoons oil
2 tablespoons flour
300 ml (½ pint) milk
50 g (2 oz) Cheddar cheese, grated
TO FINISH:
1 tablespoon grated Parmesan cheese
1 tablespoon wholewheat breadcrumbs

Make and cook the pancakes as for Provençale Pancakes (page 43).

Place the spinach in a pan and heat gently until completely thawed. Cook for 2 minutes, then pour off any liquid. Beat in the cheeses, egg, and salt, pepper and nutmeg to taste.

Divide the filling between the pancakes, roll up and place in an oiled shallow ovenproof dish.

To make the sauce, heat the oil in a pan, remove from the heat and stir in the flour. Stir in the milk until blended, return to the heat and bring to the boil, stirring, until thickened. Remove from the heat and stir in the cheese.

Spoon the sauce over the pancakes, then sprinkle with the Parmesan cheese and breadcrumbs. Cook in a preheated moderately hot oven, 190°C (375°F), Gas Mark 5, for 15 to 20 minutes, until golden.

Serves 4

FRITTATA VERDE

350 g (12 oz) spinach
3 tablespoons oil
1 onion, chopped
6 eggs
2 tablespoons grated Parmesan cheese
½ teaspoon grated nutmeg
salt and pepper

Cook the spinach with just the water clinging to its leaves after washing, for 6 to 8 minutes. Drain well, squeeze dry, then chop finely.

Heat 1 tablespoon of the oil in a pan, add the onion and fry until softened. Mix with the spinach.

Break the eggs into a bowl, add the cheese, spinach mixture, nutmeg, and salt and pepper to taste.

Heat the remaining oil in a 23 cm (9 inch) frying pan, and the egg mixture and stir lightly until beginning to set. Cook for about 5 minutes, until the underneath is set, then invert a large plate over the pan, turn the pan over and ease the frittata onto the plate. Add a little more oil to the pan, heat it then slide the frittata back into the pan and cook until the other side is set.

Cut into wedges and serve with salad and wholewheat bread.

Serves 4

RATATOUILLE AU GRATIN

6 tablespoons olive oil
1 small aubergine, sliced
2 cloves garlic, crushed
350 g (12 oz) courgettes, sliced
1 red pepper, cored, seeded and sliced
350 g (12 oz) tomatoes, skinned and sliced
1 tablespoon chopped basil
salt and pepper
500 g (1 lb) potatoes, boiled and sliced
250 g (8 oz) Mozzarella cheese, thinly sliced

Heat half the oil in a frying pan, add the aubergine and fry on both sides until just beginning to brown, adding more oil if necessary. Remove from the pan and drain on kitchen paper.

Add the remaining oil to the pan and fry the garlic, courgettes and red pepper for 8 to 10 minutes, until softened, stirring occasionally. Add the tomatoes, basil, aubergine, and salt and pepper to taste and simmer for 10 minutes.

Place the potatoes in a shallow ovenproof dish and cover with the ratatouille. Spread evenly to the edges and arrange the cheese slices over the top. Bake in a preheated moderately hot oven, 190°C (375°F), Gas Mark 5, for 15 to 20 minutes, until the cheese begins to melt. Serve immediately.

Serves 4

SPANISH OMELET

3 tablespoons olive oil
2 onions, chopped
2 cloves garlic, crushed
1 red pepper, cored, seeded and chopped
4 eggs
salt and pepper
2 large potatoes, boiled and chopped
2 tablespoons chopped parsley

Heat 2 tablespoons of the oil in a 25 cm (10 inch) frying pan, add the onions and cook until softened. Add the garlic and red pepper; cook for 8 to 10 minutes, stirring occasionally.

Whisk the eggs, with salt and pepper to taste, in a bowl, then stir in the potatoes, parsley and fried vegetables.

Heat the remaining oil in the pan, pour in the egg mixture and spread evenly to the edge. Cook for about 5 minutes, shaking the pan to prevent the omelet sticking, until it comes away from the side of the pan.

Place the pan under a preheated moderate grill for about 3 minutes to cook the top. Slide the omelet onto a warmed serving plate and cut into wedges to serve.

Serves 4

COURGETTE ROULADE

25 g (1 oz) margarine
500 g (1 lb) courgettes, grated
4 eggs, separated
1 teaspoon chopped savory
1 tablespoon chopped parsley
salt and pepper
2 tablespoons grated Parmesan cheese

FILLING:
2 tablespoons oil
1 onion, chopped
175 g (6 oz) mushrooms, sliced
1 tablespoon wholewheat flour
120 ml (4 fl oz) milk

Melt the margarine in a pan, add the courgettes and fry for 7 to 8 minutes, stirring frequently, until coloured.

Place in a bowl with the egg yolks, herbs, and salt and pepper to taste and mix well. Whisk the egg whites until fairly stiff, fold 2 tablespoons into the courgette mixture to lighten it, then carefully fold in the rest.

Turn the mixture into a lined and greased 30 × 20 cm (12 × 8 inch) Swiss roll tin and spread evenly. Cook in a preheated moderately hot oven, 200°C (400°F), Gas Mark 6, for 10 to 15 minutes, until risen and firm.

Meanwhile, prepare the filling. Heat the oil in a pan, add the onion and fry until softened. Add the mushrooms and fry for 3 minutes. Stir in the flour, then gradually stir in the milk. Add salt and pepper to taste and simmer for 3 minutes.

Sprinkle the Parmesan cheese on a sheet of greaseproof paper. Turn the roulade out onto the paper and peel off the lining paper. Spread with the filling and roll up like a Swiss roll. Serve immediately.

Serves 4

PROVENÇALE TARTLETS

wholewheat shortcrust pastry made with 250 g (8 oz) flour (see Spinach Lattice Flan, page 42)
1 tablespoon olive oil
1 onion, chopped
1 clove garlic, crushed
1 red pepper, cored, seeded and sliced
175 g (6 oz) courgettes, thinly sliced
4 tomatoes, skinned and chopped
1 tablespoon chopped marjoram
1 tablespoon chopped basil
salt and pepper
1 egg
75 ml (3 fl oz) single cream
50 g (2 oz) Gruyère cheese, grated

Roll out the pastry on a lightly floured surface and use to line six 11 cm (4½ inch) individual flan tins. Prick the base of each and chill for 20 minutes.

Bake 'blind' in a preheated moderately hot oven, 200°C (400°F), Gas Mark 6, for 10 minutes. Remove the foil and beans.

Heat the oil in a pan, add the onion and fry until softened. Add the garlic, remaining vegetables, herbs, and salt and pepper to taste, cover and simmer for 15 minutes, then spoon into the pastry cases.

Beat the egg, cream and cheese together, seasoning with a little salt and pepper, and pour over the filling. Lower the oven temperature to 190°C (375°F), Gas Mark 5, and cook the tartlets for 15 to 20 minutes, until set.

Makes 6

LENTIL AND TOMATO QUICHE

cheese pastry made with 175 g (6 oz) flour (see Broccoli and Cheese Flan, page 54)
2 tablespoons oil
2 onions, chopped
2 celery sticks, chopped
1 clove garlic, crushed
175 g (6 oz) green lentils
1 × 397 g (14 oz) can chopped tomatoes
250 ml (8 fl oz) water
salt and pepper
3 tablespoons chopped parsley
75 g (3 oz) Cheddar cheese, grated
1 tablespoon sesame seeds

Roll out the pastry on a lightly floured surface and use to line a 20 cm (8 inch) flan dish. Prick the base with a fork and chill for 20 minutes.

Bake 'blind' in a preheated moderately hot oven, 200°C (400°F), Gas Mark 6, for 10 to 12 minutes. Remove the foil and beans and return to the oven for 5 minutes.

Meanwhile, heat the oil in a pan, add the onions, celery and garlic and fry until softened. Add the lentils, tomatoes with their juice, water, and salt and pepper to taste. Cover and simmer for 1 hour, stirring occasionally, until the lentils are tender. Stir in the parsley and turn into the flan case. Sprinkle with the cheese and sesame seeds and return to the oven for 10 to 15 minutes, until the cheese is brown and bubbling.

Serves 4

LENTIL AND MUSHROOM AU GRATIN

2 tablespoons oil
1 onion, chopped
1 carrot, chopped
2 celery sticks, chopped
1 clove garlic, crushed
250 g (8 oz) red lentils
600 ml (1 pint) water
*2 tablespoons shoyu**
salt and pepper

MUSHROOM FILLING:
25 g (1 oz) margarine
250 g (8 oz) flat mushrooms, sliced
2 cloves garlic, crushed
3 tablespoons chopped parsley

TO FINISH:
75 g (3 oz) Cheddar cheese, grated

Heat the oil in a pan, add the onion, carrot and celery and fry gently for 10 minutes, until softened. Add the remaining ingredients, with salt and pepper to taste. Cover and simmer for 50 minutes to 1 hour, stirring occasionally, until the lentils are tender.

Meanwhile, prepare the filling. Melt the margarine in a frying pan, add the mushrooms and fry for 2 minutes, stirring. Add the garlic, parsley, and salt and pepper to taste and mix well.

Place half the lentil mixture in an oiled shallow ovenproof dish. Spread the mushrooms over the top, then cover with the remaining lentil mixture. Top with the cheese and bake in a preheated moderately hot oven, 190°C (375°F), Gas Mark 5, for 20 to 25 minutes until golden and bubbling.

Serve with salad and crusty bread.

Serves 4

CHEESE AND LENTIL GRATIN

1 tablespoon oil
1 onion, chopped
1 carrot, chopped
1 celery stick, chopped
175 g (6 oz) red lentils
450 ml (¾ pint) water
1 clove garlic, crushed
salt and pepper
2 tablespoons fresh wholewheat breadcrumbs
125 g (4 oz) Cheddar cheese, grated
2 tablespoons chopped parsley
1 egg, beaten
2 tablespoons sesame seeds
parsley sprigs to garnish (optional)

Heat the oil in a pan, add the onion and fry until softened. Add the carrot, celery, lentils, water, garlic, and salt and pepper to taste. Cover, bring to the boil, then lower the heat and simmer gently for about 20 minutes, until all the water is absorbed.

Add three quarters of the cheese, the parsley and egg to the lentil mixture. Stir until thoroughly mixed. Spoon the mixture into a 1 litre (1½ pint) shallow ovenproof dish and smooth the top.

Sprinkle the sesame seeds and remaining cheese over the top. Bake in a preheated moderate oven, 180°C (350°F), Gas Mark 4, for 45 minutes, until the topping is crisp and golden brown.

Garnish with parsley and serve hot with Tomato Sauce (see page 93), new potatoes and a seasonal green vegetable.

This tasty gratin is also excellent served cold with a crisp green salad.

Serves 6

LENTIL MOUSSAKA

150 ml (¼ pint) oil
1 onion, chopped
4 celery sticks, chopped
1 clove garlic, crushed
1 × 397 g (14 oz) can tomatoes
250 g (8 oz) green lentils
*2 tablespoons shoyu**
¼ teaspoon pepper
900 ml (1½ pints) water
500 g (1 lb) aubergines
salt
TOPPING:
2 eggs, beaten
150 ml (¼ pint) fromage blanc
TO FINISH:
2 tablespoons grated Parmesan cheese

Heat 1 tablespoon of the oil in a pan, add the onion and cook until softened. Add the celery, garlic, tomatoes with their juice, lentils, shoyu, pepper and water. Cover and simmer for 50 minutes, until cooked.

Meanwhile, slice the aubergines, sprinkle with salt and leave in a colander for 1 hour. Drain and pat dry with kitchen paper.

Heat some of the remaining oil in a frying pan, add the aubergines in batches and cook on both sides until golden; add more oil as required. Drain on kitchen paper.

Cover the base of a shallow ovenproof dish with the lentil mixture and arrange a layer of aubergine slices on top. Repeat the layers, finishing with aubergines.

Mix the topping ingredients with salt and pepper to taste, and pour over the aubergines. Top with the cheese and bake in a preheated moderate oven, 180°C (350°F), Gas Mark 4, for 30 to 40 minutes, until golden.

Serves 4

PROVENÇALE BEAN STEW

350 g (12 oz) haricot beans or pinto beans, soaked overnight
salt and pepper
2 tablespoons olive oil
2 onions, sliced
1 red pepper, cored, seeded and sliced
1 green pepper, cored, seeded and sliced
2 cloves garlic, crushed
1 × 397 g (14 oz) can chopped tomatoes
2 tablespoons tomato purée
1 teaspoon chopped marjoram
1 bouquet garni
50 g (2 oz) black olives, halved and stoned
2 tablespoons chopped parsley

Drain the beans, place in a pan and cover with cold water. Bring to the boil, boil rapidly for 10 minutes, then cover and simmer for 1 to 1¼ hours, until almost tender, adding a pinch of salt towards the end of cooking. Drain, reserving 300 ml (½ pint) of the liquid.

Heat the oil in a pan, add the onions and fry until softened. Add the peppers and garlic and fry gently for 10 minutes. Add the tomatoes with their juice, tomato purée, herbs, beans, reserved liquid, and salt and pepper to taste. Cover and simmer for 45 minutes, adding the olives and parsley 5 minutes before the end of the cooking time. Remove the bouquet garni.

Serve with garlic bread and salad.

Serves 4

FASOLIA

Fasolia is widely eaten in Greece. It is usually served as a vegetable dish, either hot or cold, but with the addition of more water and further seasoning, if necessary, it can also be served as a soup.

4 tablespoons olive oil
1 large onion, chopped
1 clove garlic, crushed
250 g (8 oz) haricot beans, soaked overnight
1 bouquet garni
1 tablespoon tomato purée
4 tomatoes, skinned and chopped
600 ml (1 pint) water
salt and pepper
2 teaspoons lemon juice
TO FINISH:
thinly sliced onion rings
coarsely chopped parsley

Heat the oil in a pan, add the onion and fry until pale golden. Add the garlic, drained beans, bouquet garni, tomato purée and tomatoes, then pour over the water. Bring to the boil, boil for 10 minutes, then cover and simmer for 1¾ hours or until the beans are tender, adding salt and pepper to taste towards the end of the cooking time; the liquid should be the consistency of a thick sauce. Remove the bouquet garni.

Add the lemon juice, check the seasoning and turn into a warmed serving dish. Garnish with the onion rings and parsley.

Serves 4

TANDOORI CUTLETS

250 g (8 oz) black-eyed beans, soaked overnight
2 cloves garlic, crushed
*1 tablespoon shoyu**
2 teaspoons tandoori spice mixture
2 tablespoons chopped coriander
8 spring onions, chopped
2 carrots, grated
salt and pepper
oil for shallow-frying
COATING:
1 teaspoon tandoori spice mixture
50 g (2 oz) wholewheat breadcrumbs

Drain the beans, place in a pan and cover with cold water. Bring to the boil, boil rapidly for 10 minutes, then cover and simmer for 20 to 25 minutes, until tender. Drain well, then mash.

Add the remaining ingredients, with salt and pepper to taste, and mix well.

Shape into 8 ovals and flatten to about 1 cm (½ inch) thick. Mix the tandoori spice mixture with the breadcrumbs and use to coat the cutlets completely. Fry in hot shallow oil for 4 minutes on each side. Serve hot.

Serves 4

MIXED BEAN CASSEROLE

175 g (6 oz) red kidney beans, soaked overnight
175 g (6 oz) butter beans, soaked overnight
2 tablespoons oil
2 onions, sliced
2 celery sticks, sliced
2 carrots, sliced
2 cloves garlic, crushed
1 tablespoon wholewheat flour
1 × 397 g (14 oz) can chopped tomatoes
1 tablespoon tomato purée
1 bouquet garni
salt and pepper
TOPPING:
1 small wholewheat French stick
50 g (2 oz) margarine
1 clove garlic, crushed
1 tablespoon chopped parsley
1 tablespoon sesame seeds

Drain the beans, place in separate pans and cover with cold water. Bring to the boil, boil rapidly for 10 minutes, then cover and simmer for 1 hour, or until tender. Drain, reserving 150 ml (¼ pint) of the liquid.

Heat oil in a flameproof casserole, add the onions and fry until softened. Add celery, carrots and garlic and fry for 3 to 4 minutes. Stir in the flour. Add remaining ingredients, with the beans, reserved liquid, salt and pepper to taste. Cover and cook in a preheated moderate oven, 180°C (350°F), Gas Mark 4, for 1 hour. Discard bouquet garni. Increase temperature to 200°C (400°F), Gas Mark 6.

Meanwhile, prepare the topping. Cut the French stick into 1 cm (½ inch) diagonal slices. Mix together the margarine, garlic, parsley, and salt and pepper to taste and spread on one side of each piece of bread.

Arrange plain side down to cover the top of the casserole. Sprinkle with the sesame seeds and return to the oven for 20 minutes.

Serves 4

BLACK BEAN CURRY

500 g (1 lb) black beans, soaked overnight
salt
3 tablespoons oil
2 onions, sliced
2 teaspoons ground cumin
2 teaspoons ground coriander
1 teaspoon garam masala
1 teaspoon chilli powder
1 cm (½ inch) piece root ginger, peeled and finely chopped
4 cloves garlic, crushed
1 × 397 g (14 oz) can tomatoes
3 celery sticks, sliced
1 teaspoon cardamom seeds
1 tablespoon chopped coriander

Drain the beans, place in a pan and cover with cold water. Bring to the boil, boil rapidly for 10 minutes, then cover and simmer for 1½ hours, until almost tender, adding a pinch of salt towards the end of the cooking time. Drain, reserving 300 ml (½ pint) of the liquid.

Heat the oil in a pan, add the onions and fry until softened. Add the cumin, ground coriander, garam masala, chilli powder, ginger and garlic and fry for 1 minute, stirring constantly. Add the reserved liquid, beans, tomatoes with their juice, celery, cardamom seeds, and salt to taste. Cover and simmer for 45 minutes, then stir in the chopped coriander. Serve with brown rice and Cucumber Raita (see page 50).

Serves 4

WALNUT AND LENTIL LOAF

1 tablespoon oil
1 onion, chopped
1 clove garlic, crushed
2 celery sticks, sliced
175 g (6 oz) green lentils
450 ml (¾ pint) water
125 g (4 oz) walnuts, ground
50 g (2 oz) wholewheat breadcrumbs
2 tablespoons chopped parsley
*1 tablespoon shoyu**
1 egg, beaten
salt and pepper
thyme sprigs to garnish

Heat the oil in a pan, add the onion and fry until softened. Add the garlic, celery, lentils and water and bring to the boil. Cover and simmer gently for 50 to 60 minutes, until the lentils are tender, stirring occasionally and removing the lid for the last 10 minutes to allow the moisture to evaporate.

Mix in the walnuts, breadcrumbs, parsley, shoyu, egg, and salt and pepper to taste, and mix thoroughly.

Line a 500 g (1 lb) loaf tin with foil to cover the bottom and long sides. Brush with oil. Spoon the mixture into the tin, cover with foil and bake in a preheated moderately hot oven, 190°C (375°F), Gas Mark 5, for 45 to 50 minutes.

Leave in the tin for 2 minutes, then loosen with a knife and turn out onto a warmed serving dish. Garnish with thyme and serve with Piquant Sauce (see page 93).

Serves 6

HAZELNUT AND VEGETABLE LOAF

2 tablespoons oil
1 onion, chopped
1 clove garlic, crushed
2 celery sticks, chopped
1 tablespoon wholewheat flour
175 ml (6 fl oz) tomato juice
125 g (4 oz) hazelnuts, ground and browned
125 g (4 oz) wholewheat breadcrumbs
2 carrots, grated
*1 tablespoon shoyu**
2 tablespoons chopped parsley
1 egg, beaten
salt and pepper

Heat the oil in a pan, add the onion and fry until softened. Add the garlic and celery and fry for 5 minutes, stirring occasionally. Mix in the flour, then stir in the tomato juice until thickened.

Place the remaining ingredients, with salt and pepper to taste, in a bowl and add the tomato mixture, stirring until blended.

Turn into a lined and greased 500 g (1 lb) loaf tin, cover with foil and bake in a preheated moderate oven, 180°C (350°F), Gas Mark 4, for 1 hour.

Turn out onto a warmed serving dish and serve hot with Tomato Sauce (see page 93), or cold with a mixed salad.

Serves 4

PEANUT AND MUSHROOM ROAST

3 tablespoons oil
1 onion, chopped
2 celery sticks, chopped
2 cloves garlic, crushed
250 g (8 oz) peanut kernels, ground
125 g (4 oz) wholewheat breadcrumbs
250 g (8 oz) potato, boiled and mashed
1 size 1 egg, beaten
*1 tablespoon shoyu**
1 tablespoon tomato purée
2 tablespoons chopped parsley
salt and pepper
250 g (8 oz) mushrooms, sliced
coriander leaves to garnish

Heat 1 tablespoon of the oil in a pan, add the onion, celery and garlic and fry until softened.

Mix the peanuts and breadcrumbs together in a bowl. Add the fried vegetables, potato, egg, shoyu, tomato purée, parsley, and salt and pepper to taste and mix thoroughly.

Heat the remaining oil in a pan, add the mushrooms and fry for 2 minutes, stirring.

Grease a 1 kg (2 lb) loaf tin and press in half the nut mixture. Cover with the mushrooms, then press the remaining nut mixture on top.

Cover with foil and bake in a preheated moderate oven, 180°C (350°F), Gas Mark 4, for about 1 hour.

Leave in the tin for 5 minutes, then turn out onto a warmed serving dish. Garnish with coriander and serve with Mushroom Sauce (see page 93).

Serves 4 to 6

NUT CROQUETTES

1 tablespoon oil
1 onion, chopped
1 celery stick, chopped
1 clove garlic, crushed
75 g (3 oz) mushrooms, chopped
2 teaspoons ground coriander
2 tablespoons plain flour
150 ml (1/4 pint) water
*1 tablespoon shoyu**
125 g (4 oz) cashew nuts, ground
125 g (4 oz) wholewheat breadcrumbs
2 tablespoons chopped parsley
salt and pepper
wholewheat flour to coat
oil for shallow-frying

Heat the oil in a pan, add the onion and fry until softened. Add the celery, garlic and mushrooms and fry for 5 minutes, stirring occasionally. Add the coriander and fry for 1 minute, then stir in the flour. Remove from the heat and stir in the water and shoyu until thickened. Add the cashew nuts, breadcrumbs and parsley, and salt and pepper to taste and mix well. Divide the mixture into 8 pieces, using dampened hands, then shape into croquettes.

Place the flour in a plastic bag, add the croquettes one at a time and shake until well coated. Fry in hot shallow oil for 2 minutes on each side, until golden brown and crisp. Serve with Tomato Sauce (see page 93).

Serves 4

KIWI AND GINGER SALAD

1 Ogen melon, halved and seeded
2 kiwi fruit, thinly sliced
250 g (8 oz) green grapes, halved and pipped
15 g (½ oz) stem ginger, thinly sliced
2 tablespoons ginger syrup (from the ginger)
4 tablespoons apple juice

Scoop the flesh from the melon halves with a melon baller, or cut into cubes, and place in a bowl with the kiwi fruit, grapes and ginger.

Mix the ginger syrup and apple juice together and pour over the fruit. Serve in individual dishes.

Serves 4

APPLE AND GRANOLA CRUNCH

500 g (1 lb) dessert apples, peeled, cored and chopped
125 g (4 oz) dates, chopped
300 ml (½ pint) apple juice
½ teaspoon ground cinnamon
142 ml (5 fl oz) double cream, whipped
75 g (3 oz) Granola (see page 86)

Place the apples, dates, apple juice and cinnamon in a pan, cover and cook for 10 to 15 minutes, until the apples are soft. Mash with a fork, replace the lid and leave to cool.

Spoon half the mixture into 4 glass serving dishes, top each with half the cream, then sprinkle with three quarters of the granola. Repeat the layers, finishing with the remaining granola.

Serves 4

STRAWBERRY CHEESE WITH ALMOND FINGERS

ALMOND FINGERS:
125 g (4 oz) margarine
50 g (2 oz) Muscovado or soft dark brown sugar
125 g (4 oz) wholewheat flour
50 g (2 oz) ground almonds, toasted
25 g (1 oz) blanched almonds, chopped
STRAWBERRY CHEESE:
2 tablespoons clear honey
175 g (6 oz) strawberries
175 g (6 oz) curd cheese

Cream the margarine and sugar together until light and fluffy. Add the flour and ground almonds and stir until the mixture binds together.

Roll out the dough to an oblong and press into an 18 × 28 cm (7 × 11 inch) baking tin. Flatten with a palette knife and prick with a fork, then sprinkle with the chopped almonds and press in lightly. Bake in a preheated moderate oven, 180°C (350°F), Gas Mark 4, for 30 to 35 minutes until pale golden. Allow to cool slightly, then mark into 20 fingers. Cool completely before removing from the tin.

Place the honey and half of the strawberries in an electric blender or food processor and work to a purée. Beat the cheese until smooth, then fold in the fruit purée. Slice the remaining strawberries, set aside 4 slices for decoration and divide the rest between individual dishes.

Spoon the strawberry cheese into the dishes, decorate with the reserved strawberry slices and serve with the almond fingers.

Serves 4

NOTE: Store any leftover almond fingers in an airtight tin.

HIGHLAND CREAM

25 g (1 oz) blanched almonds, chopped
25 g (1 oz) medium oatmeal
25 g (1 oz) wholewheat breadcrumbs
142 ml (5 fl oz) double cream
3 tablespoons whisky
2 tablespoons clear honey
150 g (5 oz) natural yogurt

Mix together the almonds, oatmeal and breadcrumbs and place on a baking sheet. Place under a preheated hot grill until golden brown, stirring frequently. Leave to cool.

Whip the cream, whisky and honey together until soft peaks form, then fold in the yogurt and the almond mixture. Spoon into individual glasses and chill until required.

Serves 6

BANANA AND APRICOT YOGURT

125 g (4 oz) dried apricots, chopped
300 g (10 oz) natural yogurt
1 banana
1 tablespoon flaked almonds, toasted

Place the apricots in a bowl with the yogurt. Mix well, then cover and leave in the refrigerator overnight.

Slice the banana and fold into the yogurt mixture. Spoon into individual glasses and sprinkle with the almonds to serve.

Serves 4

FRUIT AND NUT CRUMBLE

175 g (6 oz) dried apricots
125 g (4 oz) dried pitted prunes
125 g (4 oz) dried figs
50 g (2 oz) dried apples
600 ml (1 pint) apple juice
175 g (6 oz) wholewheat flour
75 g (3 oz) margarine
50 g (2 oz) muscovado or soft dark brown sugar, sifted
50 g (2 oz) hazelnuts, chopped

Place the dried fruits in a bowl with the apple juice and leave overnight. Transfer to a saucepan and simmer for 10 to 15 minutes, until softened. Turn into an ovenproof dish.

Place the flour in a bowl and rub in the margarine until the mixture resembles breadcrumbs. Stir in the sugar and hazelnuts, then sprinkle over the fruit.

Bake in a preheated moderately hot oven, 200°C (400°F), Gas Mark 6, for 25 to 30 minutes. Serve with Yogurt Snow (see page 80).

Serves 6

Variation: For the topping, replace the hazelnuts with toasted chopped almonds or grated coconut.

APRICOT PANCAKES

PANCAKE BATTER:
*50 g (2 oz) buckwheat flour**
50 g (2 oz) plain flour
1 egg, beaten
300 ml (½ pint) milk
1 tablespoon oil

FILLING:
350 g (12 oz) dried apricots, chopped and soaked for 2 hours
450 ml (¾ pint) apple juice

TO FINISH:
2 tablespoons clear honey
25 g (1 oz) flaked almonds, toasted

Place the flours in a bowl and make a well in the centre. Add the egg, then gradually stir in half the milk and the oil. Beat thoroughly until smooth, then add the remaining milk.

Heat a 15 cm (6 inch) omelet pan and add 1 teaspoon oil. Pour in 1 tablespoon of the batter, tilting the pan to coat the bottom evenly. Cook until the underside is brown, then turn and cook for 10 seconds. Repeat with the remaining batter, stacking the pancakes as they are cooked.

To make the filling, place the apricots and apple juice in a pan, cover and cook gently for 10 minutes.

Place a little of the filling on each pancake, roll up and arrange in an ovenproof dish. Warm the honey and spoon over the pancakes to glaze. Bake in a preheated moderate oven, 180°C (350°F), Gas Mark 4, for 10 to 15 minutes, until heated through. Sprinkle with the almonds and serve with Yogurt Snow (see page 80).

Serves 4

APPLE AND RAISIN PIE

175 g (6 oz) wholewheat flour
125 g (4 oz) plain flour, sifted
150 g (5 oz) margarine
3-4 tablespoons iced water

FILLING:

750 g (1½ lb) dessert apples, peeled, cored and thinly sliced
2 tablespoons brown sugar
1 teaspoon ground cinnamon
4 cloves
50 g (2 oz) raisins

TO FINISH:

1 tablespoon sesame seeds

Place the flours in a bowl and rub in the margarine until the mixture resembles fine breadcrumbs. Stir in enough water to mix to a fairly stiff dough.

Turn onto a floured surface, knead lightly until smooth, then divide in half. Roll out one piece thinly and use to line a shallow 20 cm (8 inch) pie dish.

Layer the apples with the sugar, spices and raisins in the pastry case. Brush the pastry rim with cold water.

Roll out the remaining pastry and use to cover the pie. Seal and pinch the edges well, then trim off any surplus pastry with a sharp knife. Make a hole in the centre of the pie and chill for 20 minutes.

Brush with water and sprinkle with the sesame seeds. Bake in a preheated moderately hot oven, 200°C (400°F), Gas Mark 6, for 30 to 40 minutes, until golden. Serve warm or cold with Yogurt Snow (see page 80).

Serves 6

DATE AND APPLE SHORTCAKE

NUT PASTRY:
75 g (3 oz) margarine
40 g (1½ oz) muscovado or soft dark brown sugar
125 g (4 oz) wholewheat flour
75 g (3 oz) brazil nuts, ground
egg white for brushing
1 tablespoon chopped brazil nuts

FILLING:
3 tablespoons apple juice
500 g (1 lb) dessert apples, peeled and cored
125 g (4 oz) dates, chopped
1 teaspoon ground cinnamon
142 ml (5 fl oz) double cream, whipped

Beat the margarine and sugar together until softened. Stir in the flour and ground nuts and mix to a firm dough. Turn onto a floured surface; knead lightly until smooth. Divide in half and roll each piece into a 20 cm (8 inch) round on a baking sheet. Brush one with egg white and sprinkle with the chopped nuts.

Bake in a preheated moderately hot oven, 190°C (375°F), Gas Mark 5, for 10 to 15 minutes, until golden. Cut the nut-covered round into 8 sections while warm. Transfer both rounds to a wire rack to cool.

Place the apple juice in a pan and slice the apples into it. Cover and cook gently for about 10 minutes, stirring occasionally, until just soft. Add the dates and cinnamon, cover and leave to cool.

Spread the apple filling over the whole shortcake round, cover with the cream, then arrange the cut triangles on top.

Serves 8

YOGURT SNOW

2 egg whites
3 tablespoons clear honey
300 g (10 oz) natural yogurt

Whisk the egg whites until stiff, then whisk in the honey and continue whisking until very thick. Carefully fold in the yogurt and serve immediately, instead of cream.
Makes about 450 ml (¾ pint)

SUMMER PUDDING

500 g (1 lb) mixed blackberries and blackcurrants
3 tablespoons clear honey
125 g (4 oz) raspberries
125 g (4 oz) strawberries
8 slices wholewheat bread, crusts removed

Place the blackberries, blackcurrants and honey in a heavy-based pan and cook gently for 10 to 15 minutes until tender, stirring occasionally. Add the raspberries and strawberries and leave to cool. Strain the fruit, reserving the juice.

Cut 3 circles of bread to fit the base, middle and top of a 900 ml (1½ pint) pudding basin. Shape the remaining bread to fit round the side of the basin. Soak all the bread in the reserved fruit juice.

Line the bottom of the basin with the smallest circle of bread, then arrange the shaped bread around the side. Pour in half the fruit and place the middle sized circle of bread on top. Cover with the remaining fruit, then top with the largest bread circle. Fold over any bread protruding from the basin.

Cover with a saucer small enough to fit inside the basin and put a 500 g (1 lb) weight on top. Leave in the refrigerator overnight.

Turn onto a serving plate, pour over any remaining fruit juice and serve with whipped cream or Yogurt Snow (above).
Serves 8

NUT CREAM

125 g (4 oz) cashew nuts
150 ml (¼ pint) milk

Place the nuts and milk in an electric blender and blend until smooth. Chill and serve instead of cream.
Makes about 150 ml (¼ pint)

CASHEW FLAPJACKS

125 g (4 oz) margarine
90 ml (3 fl oz) clear honey
1 tablespoon malt extract
250 g (8 oz) rolled oats
50 g (2 oz) cashew nuts, chopped

Place the margarine, honey and malt extract in a pan and heat gently until melted. Remove from the heat, stir in the rolled oats and cashew nuts and mix thoroughly. Turn into a greased shallow 18 × 28 cm (7 × 11 inch) tin and smooth the top with a palette knife.

Bake in a preheated moderate oven, 180°C (350°F), Gas Mark 4, for 25 to 30 minutes.

Cool in the tin for 2 minutes, then cut into fingers. Allow to cool completely before removing the flapjacks from the tin.

Makes 20

MUESLI BISCUITS

125 g (4 oz) butter or margarine
90 ml (3 fl oz) clear honey
350 g (10 oz) muesli
2 tablespoons sunflower seeds

Place the butter or margarine and honey in a large pan and heat gently until melted. Remove from the heat, stir in the muesli and sunflower seeds and mix thoroughly.

Spoon mounds of the mixture onto lightly greased baking sheets, spacing them well apart and flatten with a palette knife.

Bake in a preheated moderately hot oven, 190°C (375°F), Gas Mark 5, for 10 to 12 minutes until golden brown. Leave for 3 minutes, then loosen the biscuits with a palette knife and leave on the baking sheets until completely cool.

Makes 16

NOTE: The sweetness of these delicious biscuits will depend on the type of muesli used. If you use an unsweetened variety, add 1 to 2 tablespoons raw sugar, according to taste.

APRICOT AND NUT TEABREAD

125 g (4 oz) All-Bran
50 g (2 oz) muscovado sugar
75 g (3 oz) dried apricots, snipped
300 ml (½ pint) apple juice
125 g (4 oz) wholewheat flour
2 teaspoons baking powder, sifted
50 g (2 oz) hazelnuts, chopped

Place the All-Bran, sugar, apricots and apple juice in a mixing bowl and leave to soak for 1 hour.

Stir the flour, baking powder and all but 1 tablespoon of the chopped hazelnuts into the apricot mixture and beat thoroughly.

Turn into a lined and greased 500 g (1 lb) loaf tin. Sprinkle the remaining nuts over the top and bake in a preheated moderate oven, 180°C (350°F), Gas Mark 4, for 55 to 60 minutes.

Turn onto a wire rack to cool. Cut into slices to serve.

Makes one 500 g (1 lb) loaf

FIGGY PRUNE CAKE

125 g (4 oz) pitted prunes, chopped
125 g (4 oz) dried figs, chopped
150 ml (1/4 pint) apple juice
90 ml (3 fl oz) clear honey
120 ml (4 fl oz) corn oil
2 eggs, beaten
150 g (5 oz) wholewheat flour
1/2 teaspoon bicarbonate of soda
1 teaspoon ground mixed spice
1/2 teaspoon ground nutmeg
120 ml (4 fl oz) natural yogurt
25 g (1 oz) walnuts, chopped

Place the prunes and figs in a pan with the apple juice, cover and simmer gently for 10 minutes. Leave to cool. Stir in the remaining ingredients, except the walnuts, and mix thoroughly.

Pour into a lined and greased deep 20 cm (8 inch) cake tin and sprinkle the walnuts over the top. Bake in a preheated moderate oven, 180°C (350°F), Gas Mark 4, for 50 to 55 minutes, until firm to the touch. Leave in the tin for 2 minutes, then turn onto a wire rack to cool.

Makes one 20 cm (8 inch) cake

GRANOLA

120 ml (4 fl oz) safflower oil
90 ml (3 fl oz) malt extract
90 ml (3 fl oz) clear honey
250 g (8 oz) rolled oats
250 g (8 oz) jumbo oats (large oat flakes)
125 g (4 oz) hazelnuts
25 g (1 oz) desiccated coconut
50 g (2 oz) sunflower seeds
25 g (1 oz) sesame seeds

Place the oil, malt and honey in a large pan and heat gently until the malt is runny. Mix in the remaining ingredients and stir thoroughly.

Turn into a large roasting pan and bake in a preheated moderately hot oven, 190°C (375°F), Gas Mark 5, for 30 to 35 minutes, stirring occasionally. Leave to cool, then separate the pieces with your fingers.

Store in an airtight container. Serve with natural yogurt at breakfast time, or use as a topping for stewed fruits.

Makes 1 kg (2 lb)

GRANARY LOAF

250 g (8 oz) granary flour
250 g (8 oz) wholewheat flour
1 teaspoon salt
15 g (½ oz) fresh yeast
300 ml (½ pint) warm water
1 tablespoon malt extract
1 tablespoon oil
cracked wheat for sprinkling

Mix the flours and salt together in a bowl. Cream the yeast with a little of the water and leave until frothy. Add to the flour with the remaining water, malt and oil and mix to a dough.

Turn onto a floured surface. Knead for 5 minutes, until smooth and elastic. Place in a clean bowl, cover with a damp cloth and leave to rise in a warm place until doubled in size.

Turn onto a floured surface and knead for a few minutes. Shape into an 18 cm (7 inch) round and flatten slightly. Place on a greased baking sheet. Brush with water and sprinkle with cracked wheat. Cover and leave to rise in a warm place for about 30 minutes, until almost doubled in size.

Bake in a preheated hot oven, 220°C (425°F), Gas Mark 7, for 25 to 30 minutes or until the bread sounds hollow when tapped underneath. Cool on a wire rack.

Makes 1 granary loaf

Granary Rolls: Divide the risen dough into 10 equal pieces. Knead each piece into a round and place on a floured baking sheet. Cover and leave to rise until doubled in size. Bake as above for 10 to 15 minutes.

WHOLEWHEAT BREAD

1.5 kg (3 lb) wholewheat flour
1 tablespoon salt
25 g (1 oz) fresh yeast
900 ml (1½ pints) warm water
2 tablespoons malt extract
2 tablespoons oil
1 tablespoon sesame seeds

Mix the flour and salt together in a bowl. Mix the yeast with a little of the water and leave until frothy. Add to the flour with the remaining water, malt extract and oil. Mix to a dough.

Turn onto a floured surface and knead for 8 to 10 minutes, until smooth and elastic. Place in a clean bowl, cover with a damp cloth and leave to rise in a warm place for about 2 hours, until doubled in size.

Turn onto a floured surface, knead for a few minutes, then divide into 2 pieces. Shape and place in greased 1 kg (2 lb) loaf tins. Brush with water and sprinkle with the sesame seeds.

Cover and leave to rise in a warm place for about 30 minutes, until the dough just reaches the top of the tins. Bake in a preheated hot oven, 220°C (425°F), Gas Mark 7, for 15 minutes, then lower the temperature to 190°C (375°F), Gas Mark 5, and bake for a further 20 to 25 minutes, until the bread sounds hollow when tapped underneath. Turn onto a wire rack to cool.

Makes two 1 kg (2 lb) loaves

Wholewheat Baps: Use ½ quantity dough, replacing half the water with warm milk. Divide the risen dough into 12 equal pieces. Knead each piece into a ball, then roll into a 10 cm (4 inch) round and place on floured baking sheets. Sprinkle with sesame seeds or flour. Cover and leave to rise until doubled in size. Bake in a preheated hot oven, 220°C (425°F), Gas Mark 7, for 10 to 15 minutes. Cool on a wire rack.

SESAME THINS

175 g (6 oz) wholewheat flour
50 g (2 oz) medium oatmeal
pinch of salt
1 teaspoon baking powder
75 g (3 oz) margarine
1 tablespoon malt extract
2 tablespoons milk
25 g (1 oz) sesame seeds

Place the flour, oatmeal and salt in a mixing bowl and sift in the baking powder; mix well. Rub in the margarine until the mixture resembles breadcrumbs.

Whisk the malt and milk together until blended, then add to the dry ingredients with the sesame seeds. Mix to a firm dough.

Turn onto a floured surface and roll out thinly. Cut into 6 cm (2½ inch) rounds with a plain cutter.

Place on a baking sheet and bake in a preheated moderately hot oven, 190°C (375°F), Gas Mark 5, for 12 to 15 minutes, until golden. Transfer to a wire rack to cool. Serve with cheese.

Makes 20 to 24

LIGHT RYE BREAD

250 g (8 oz) rye flour
500 g (1 lb) wholewheat flour
2 teaspoons fine sea salt
15 g (½ oz) fresh yeast
450 ml (¾ pint) warm water
2 tablespoons molasses
2 tablespoons oil
milk for brushing
1 teaspoon caraway seeds

Mix the flours and salt together in a bowl. Cream the yeast with a little of the water and leave until frothy. Add to the flour mixture with the remaining water, molasses and oil and mix thoroughly to a soft dough.

Turn onto a floured surface and knead for 5 minutes, until smooth and elastic. Place in a clean bowl, cover with a damp cloth and leave to rise in a warm place for about 2 hours, until doubled in size.

Turn onto a floured surface and knead for a few minutes. Shape into 2 oval loaves and place on greased baking sheets. Prick with a fork in 8 or 9 places, then leave to rise in a warm place for 30 minutes, until doubled in size.

Brush with milk, sprinkle with the caraway seeds and bake in a preheated hot oven, 220°C (425°F), Gas Mark 7, for 10 minutes. Lower the heat to 190°C (375°F), Gas Mark 5, and bake for a further 25 to 30 minutes, until the loaves sound hollow when tapped underneath. Cool on a wire rack.

Makes 2 loaves

Buckwheat Plait: Use buckwheat flour* instead of rye flour.

To shape the plait, cut the dough in half, then cut each half into 3 equal pieces. Shape the pieces into long thin 'sausages'. Take 3 'sausages', moisten one end of each with water and press together; plait, dampening the ends to join. Repeat with the remaining 3 'sausages' to make 2 loaves. Sprinkle with 1 teaspoon whole buckwheat* instead of caraway seeds.

Leave to rise in a warm place for 30 minutes, until doubled in size. Bake in a preheated hot oven, 220°C (425°F), Gas Mark 7, for 10 minutes, then lower the heat to 190°C (375°F), Gas Mark 5, and bake for a further 15 to 20 minutes. Cool on a wire rack.

DRESSINGS AND SAUCES

SHOYU DRESSING

175 ml (6 fl oz) oil
*2 tablespoons shoyu**
2 tablespoons lemon juice
2 cloves garlic
pepper

Place all the ingredients in a screw-topped jar and shake well to blend.
Makes 300 ml (½ pint)

Ginger Dressing: Add a 2.5 cm (1 inch) piece finely chopped root ginger to the ingredients.

FRENCH DRESSING

175 ml (6 fl oz) olive oil
4 tablespoons wine vinegar
1 teaspoon Meaux mustard
1 clove garlic, crushed
1 teaspoon clear honey
salt and pepper

Put all the ingredients in a screw-topped jar, adding salt and pepper to taste. Shake well before serving.
Makes 250 ml (8 fl oz)

Vinaigrette Dressing: Add 2 tablespoons chopped mixed herbs – such as mint, parsley, chives, chervil or thyme – to the above ingredients.

GREEN HERB DRESSING

25 g (1 oz) parsley
15 g (½ oz) mint
15 g (½ oz) chives
3 sorrel leaves, chopped
150 g (5 oz) natural yogurt
2 tablespoons olive oil
juice of ½ lemon
1 teaspoon clear honey
½ teaspoon salt
¼ teaspoon pepper

Remove the stalks from the parsley and mint. Place the leaves in an electric blender or food processor with the remaining ingredients and blend until smooth.

Store in the refrigerator for up to one week. Shake before use.
Makes 300 ml (½ pint)

TOMATO SAUCE

2 tablespoons olive oil
1 onion, chopped
1 clove garlic, crushed
500 g (1 lb) tomatoes, skinned and chopped
150 ml (¼ pint) vegetable stock
2 teaspoons tomato purée
1 bay leaf
salt and pepper

Heat the oil in a pan, add the onion and fry for 5 minutes, until softened. Add the remaining ingredients, with salt and pepper to taste, cover and simmer for 20 minutes, stirring occasionally.

Cool slightly and remove the bay leaf. Work in an electric blender or food processor until smooth, or rub through a sieve. Reheat gently.

Makes 350 ml (12 fl oz)

MUSHROOM SAUCE

2 tablespoons oil
1 onion, chopped
1 clove garlic, crushed
125 g (4 oz) mushrooms, chopped
1 tablespoon wholewheat flour
75 ml (3 fl oz) vegetable stock
75 ml (3 fl oz) milk
*2 teaspoons shoyu**
salt and pepper

Heat the oil in a pan, add the onion and fry until softened. Add the garlic and mushrooms and cook for about 2 minutes. Stir in the flour, then remove from the heat and stir in the stock and milk. Bring to the boil, stirring, and cook for 3 minutes. Stir in the shoyu, and seasoning to taste.

Cool slightly, then work in an electric blender or food processor until smooth. Reheat gently.

Serve with nut roasts and rissoles.

Makes 450 ml (¾ pint)

PIQUANT SAUCE

150 g (5 oz) natural yogurt
1 teaspoon tomato purée
½ teaspoon cumin powder
1 teaspoon ground coriander
1 teaspoon clear honey

Place all the ingredients in a small bowl and mix together thoroughly.

Makes 150 ml (¼ pint)

INDEX